Disney

FROZEN FEVER
PARTY BOOK

EDDA USA

DISNEY FROZEN FEVER PARTY BOOK

© 2015 Disney Enterprises, Inc.

Authors: Olafur Gunnar Gudlaugsson, Olina Thorvaldsdottir
Photographer: Gassi.is
Layout and design: Olafur Gunnar Gudlaugsson
Cover design: Olafur Gunnar Gudlaugsson
Editor: Tinna Proppe, tinna@eddausa.com
Printing: Printed in Canada

Distributed by Midpoint Book Sales & Distribution

ISBN: 978-1-94078-725-1

www.eddausa.com

Welcome

You are cordially invited to help plan and throw the best *Frozen Fever* party of the year... perhaps even of all time!

In this book we say that every party starts with an invitation but the truth is that every party starts with planning! Luckily, the planning and preparation is almost as fun as the party itself.

Choosing the cakes and decorations, sending out the invitations, planning the games and all the other fantastic details are what will make your *Frozen Fever* party an instant success. And everything you need to pull it off can be found in this *Frozen Fever* Party Book!

Dive in, start planning, and have fun!

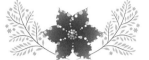

Invitations

A party always starts with an invitation and for the perfect *Frozen Fever* party you need a fitting invite! If you want to use your time baking you can always find simple invitation templates but if you want to go all out, take a look at some more elaborate ideas on the next few pages!

Arendelle Party Invitation

If anything might be called an official Arendelle invitation, this might be it!

STEP 1

The original Arendelle Party Invitation can be found on page 60.

STEP 2

Take the template to a shop that provides professional photocopies in your neighborhood. Be careful not to lose the page or tear it if you remove it from the book, since there are other templates on it that you will also need. It is preferable to take the whole book with you to make the copies. The professionals know how to make a good photocopy and will take care of the book.

YOU ARE INVITED TO _____ FROZEN FEVER PARTY!

WHEN _____

WHERE _____

RSVP _____

STEP 3

The width of the invitation template is 7½ inches. Have copies of your invitation made to fit in the specific envelope you have chosen. The photocopy professional may even have envelopes to choose from. You can also treat the invitation like a post card and just put the mailing address and stamp on the reverse side and pop it in the mail. Simple as that!

STEP 4

It's a good idea to order extra photocopies in case any mistakes are made when filling in all the information for your guests.

Have fun!

Elsa's Jewel Invitation

Elsa loves surprises and the surprise in this invitation is no exception. A beautiful jewel is hidden within it that might even serve as a game prop later on!

WHAT YOU NEED

Various kinds of threadable plastic pearls and stones

Plastic thread

Soft giftwrap paper

Cellophane

Thin colored ribbons

Flower cutout (p. 60)

2-ply colored paper

STEP 1

Create wristbands, as many as needed, using standard threadable plastic pearls and plastic thread. Be creative and use your imagination. Do not close at the ends. This will be done when the guests arrive (see page 52)

STEP 2

Place the wristband on soft giftwrap paper. Wrap the paper around the wristband and tape firmly. Include a message instructing the guest to bring the wristband along to your party.

STEP 3

Make an invitation, using one of the flower templates on page 60 and 2-ply colored paper. Color and illustrate as desired on one side and write out the invitation on the blank side.

STEP 4

Wrap cellophane over the giftwrap paper, gather together and fasten it with a ribbon. Thread one loose end of the ribbon through your flower invitation to secure it to the package and finish it off with a bow.

Spring in a Bottle Invitation

If you want to do something a little different and creative, this invitation is for you! A bottle filled with the flowers of Arendelle spring and a personal invitation to your party!

WHAT YOU NEED

Plastic jars with screwable lids

See-through paper

Silver glitter

Colored marker

Flowers
(preferably spring flowers)

Colored ribbons

Flower cutout (p. 60)

2-ply colored paper

STEP 1

Write out the invitation on see-through paper with a colored marker. Be sure to measure the paper so it will fit neatly into the jar. Use any colored marker except black.

STEP 2

Add some glitter for a sparkling effect by sprinkling it over the invitation.

YOU ARE INVITED TO ANGELA'S 10TH BIRTHDAY!! RSV

Step 3

Place the invitation in the jar by rolling it neatly up and placing it gently in the middle of it. The paper will then fold out to the sides of the jar

Step 4

Put the flowers into the jar. These can be any flowers you can find, but spring flowers are preferable for this specific invitation.

Step 5

Another option is to have the invitation on the outside of the jar.

Make a flower decoration using one of the templates on page 60 and 2-ply colored paper. Color and illustrate as desired on one or both sides. Write out the invitation and finaly make a hole in the decoration and thread with a ribbon.

Tie the ribbon around the lid and make a beautiful bow. Make as many Spring in a Bottle invitations as needed.

Anna's Sunflower Invitation

This invitation will put a smile on everyone's face!
A simple yet beautiful design based on a beautiful sunflower!

WHAT YOU NEED

2-ply
white paper
(non coated & matte)

Gouache paints

Paintbrush

Colored pencil

Sunflower
template (p. 61)

Fixative

STEP 1

Make photocopies of the sunflower template on page 61, using thick 2-ply white paper (see instructions for photocopying templates on page 6). Copy as many as needed.

STEP 2

Color the individual elements as shown on the picture on the right using gouache paints and water.

STEP 3

When using gouache paints it is good to keep in mind the amount of paint needed for each segment of the flower.
Start by mixing the yellow gouache with a little water. It should be runny but not too thin.

Apply the yellow paint carefully on the intended parts of the flower. Be sure not to use too much at a time. Once you have finished let it dry thoroughly. Continue with the blue parts, then the red and finish with the dark brown. Always allow the paint to dry before starting with another color. For the shade in the yellow use a light green colored pencil, using light strokes.

Once you are done, spray the artwork with some fixative to prevent smearing. Finally cut out the invitation with small scissors.

STEP 4

Use a black marker to write what is desired on the blue circle. Write the details of the invitation on the reverse side. Make sure to plot out the text with a pencil beforehand. Write lightly so there is not much erasing needed.

STEP 5

For those who don't have time for painting, simply take the fully illustrated template on page 61 to the photocopier.

Olaf's Cutout Invitation

Here is another premade template worthy of any party with an Olaf theme.

WHAT YOU NEED

- Small scissors
- Regular pencil (HH)
- Colored pens and markers

STEP 1

Take the template to a shop that provides professional photocopies in your neighborhood. If you remove the page from the book be careful not to lose it or tear it. You want to keep the book intact, so it's preferable to take the whole book with you to make the copies. The professionals know how to make a good photocopy and will take care of the book.

STEP 2

The height of the invitation template is 7$^{1/2}$ inches. Have copies of your invitation made to fit in the specific envelope you have chosen. The photocopy professional may even have envelopes to choose from. In this case you might not want an envelope; it all depends on how you want to present the invitation. You can treat it like a postcard and just put the mailing address and stamp on the reverse side and pop it in the mail. Simple as that!

STEP 3

It's a good idea to order extra photocopies in case any mistakes are made when writing in all the information for your guests.

STEP 4

Write out the invitation lightly on the blank side with a light pencil. Be sure to include all the information needed. By plotting out the text lightly you won't run out of space when writing the text. Trace over the pencils with colored pens or markers.

STEP 5

Use small scissors to cut out the invitation along the dotted lines. Once finished, fold the two halves of Olaf and you are done. Have fun!

Decorations

For Anna's party Elsa goes all out decorating the
courtyard. Even though Olaf didn't quite get the spelling
of HAPPY BIRTHDAY ANNA right we are confident
that the decorative ideas on these pages will not be too
much for you to handle! Dive in and create the perfect
Frozen Fever setting.

Sunflower Table Decoration

In *Frozen Fever*, Elsa chooses beautiful tablecloths for Anna's birthday party. Filled with sunflowers and leaves, this design is the perfect décor for any *Frozen Fever* party.

WHAT YOU NEED

Paper tablecloth

Gouache paints
(Yellow/green/brown/red)

Pencil

Paintbrush

Long ruler

Template
on p. 62-63

STEP 1

Photocopy the template on page 62-63 onto A3 paper (see complete photocopying instructions on page 6).

STEP 2

Most paper tablecloths are see-through. Start on one corner and trace the outlines of the template lightly with a pencil on the paper cloth. The template on page 62-63 does not cover the whole cloth, so you need to move the template horizontally to trace more patterns. See more detailed instructions on page 63. Note: This will take some time. To save time, try using a smaller table and have it stand in a corner. Then only two sides can be seen.

STEP 3

Color the traced pattern using different paint colors. To get an even color throughout the decoration, use one color at a time. Do all the sunflower petals, then do all the leaves. Make sure to have enough individual colors for the whole process and let the cloth dry thoroughly in between.

STEP 4

Spread the paper tablecloth over a table and then a white cotton tablecloth over it.

Olaf's Party Garland

WHAT YOU NEED

Letter sized
white paper

Different
color paint

Large
brush

Rope

Laundry
clips

Whether a birthday, a baby shower or other type of party, a garland always creates the perfect setting. You might want to check your spelling so you don't make the same mistakes as Olaf in *Frozen Fever*.

STEP 1

Find out how many letters are in the intended phrase. That is how many laundry clips and how many pieces of paper are needed. Or you can combine two letters together as seen above.

Measure the rope across the intended room and put aside for the moment.

Step 2

Paint the individual letters as needed on each piece of paper. If desired, the pages can be colored before painting the letters. If this is done use a thicker kind of paper, 2-ply or more.

Step 3

After everything has dried, attach the paper to the rope with the laundry clips and hang up the garland where desired.

Flower Coasters & Glass Decorations

Frozen Fever is all about flowers, summer and joy! Maybe that is why Olaf loves it. For coasters and glass decorations you can't go wrong with these flower inspired designs.

What You Need

2-ply colored
paper and/or cardboard

Flower templates (p.60)

Brush

Gouache paints

Colored pencils

Scissors

Silk flowers

Ribbons

Glue

The Coasters

Step 1

Copy the flower patterns on page 60 by tracing them with a pencil onto 2-ply colored paper or cardboard. No need to be too accurate. Just have fun with it.
Cut out the flowers with scissors.

STEP 2

Decorate the cutouts as desired with paint and colored pencils. Crayons can be helpful in the end. Just experiment, use your imagination and have fun.

The Glass

STEP 1

Measure and cut out two different colored ribbons. Be sure to have enough ribbon to make a bow in the end.

STEP 2

Glue the ribbons around the glass, one just above the other.

STEP 3

Tie the loose ends of the ribbons into a beautiful bow.

STEP 4

Take a silk flower and remove the plastic stem. Put a drop of glue onto the cut end of the flower and press tightly onto the middle of the bows on the glass. Hold firmly until the glue has dried.

Frozen Fever Flower Decoration

Flowers are so beautiful, including them in your party decorations will be an instant success. Use your imagination to arrange them any way you choose!

WHAT YOU NEED

All kinds of spring flowers

INSTRUCTIONS

This decoration is so much fun because ... well, anything goes!

You can arrange the flowers in a pattern or you can just spread them any way you want over the table.

They can be fresh or they can be dry, it does not matter. The only thing recommended is that you try to use mostly spring flowers; daffodils, tulips, hyacinths, primroses and many more.

And let's not forget sunflowers, which are also featured in *Frozen Fever*. They make everything look beautiful!

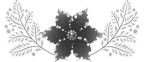

Cakes & Drinks

A three layered sunflower cake, scrumptious blue and green cupcakes, deliciously refreshing summer drinks and a decadent lemon bundt cake, all can be found in this chapter ... and with nutritious options! Even the most elaborate designs are made easy and achievable for every *Frozen Fever* party.

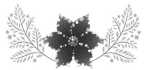

Anna's Birthday Cake

Elsa went all out planning for her sister's birthday and the main attraction was definitely the amazing three-layered sunflower cake! Here is a version inspired by that beautiful cake. It may look difficult to make, but anybody can do it!

What You Need

3 cake pans of different sizes

¾ cup dark cocoa powder

1 ¼ cups hot water

⅔ cup sour cream

2 ⅔ cups flour, plus more for dusting

2 tsp baking powder

1 tsp baking soda

½ tsp salt

¾ cup unsalted butter, softened

½ cup unflavored shortening

1 ½ cups sugar

1 cup dark brown sugar, firmly packed

3 large eggs, at room temperature

1 tbsp vanilla

Instructions

- Preheat oven to 325°F degrees.
- Butter and flour 3 cake pans, line with parchment, and butter the parchment.
- Mix cocoa powder, hot water, and sour cream together.
- Sift flour, baking soda, baking powder, and salt, in a separate bowl and set aside to cool.
- Beat butter and shortening together with your hand blender or stand mixer on medium speed until light and fluffy, about 5 minutes.
- Add sugars to the butter and shortening and beat until light and fluffy, about 5 more minutes.
- Add the eggs, 1 at a time, and then vanilla, and beat until incorporated. Then, slowly add the flour mixture and cocoa mixture separately to the batter, alternating the 2 kinds and ending with the flour.
- Divide the batter between the 3 pans and spread evenly. Bake for 35–40 minutes (rotate the pans halfway through) or until a toothpick inserted in the center of the cakes comes out clean. Let cool for 20 minutes then invert onto a rack to cool completely.
- When the cakes have cooled completely you can cut them into the size you need to make this three-layered cake. It looks best if you have the second cake an inch smaller then the bottom one.
- If you would like to have the cake bigger, double the amount in the recipe.

The Fondant for the Birthday Cake

Fondant icing, also commonly referred to simply as fondant,
is an edible icing used to decorate or sculpt cakes and pastries.
You can either make your own fondant or buy it ready-made.

WHAT YOU NEED

25 marshmallows

2½ tbsp cold water

3 cups icing sugar

Shortening
(or any kind of cooking
grease to put on the
utensils you use, your
hands and the surface on
which you are kneading
and rolling out the
fondant)

**Medium size,
microwavable bowl**

Large bowl

Sift

Spatula

Fork

Note: Use 1 tbsp cold water for every 10 marshmallows you use in the recipe. For any standard size cake you need 25 marshmallows.

INSTRUCTIONS

- In preparation for making your fondant, have all of your materials ready and have all of your utensils and the inside of your large bowl greased with shortening or the cooking grease of your choice. Add 1 cup of icing sugar to the greased bowl, and swirl it around so that the entire inside of the bowl has been coated with icing sugar.
- Put the marshmallows in the medium sized bowl and sprinkle with water. Microwave the marshmallows and water on high heat for 30 seconds, and then stir. Return the marshmallows to the microwave for another 15 seconds and stir again. Continue this process until the marshmallows are fully melted and mixed with the water.
- If you want to color the fondant it's best to do that now. Mix the color into the marshmallows, keeping in mind that the color needs to be a little bit darker than the color you'd like, as it will lighten when you incorporate the icing sugar.
- Once the melted marshmallows are your desired color, pour them into the large bowl that you have greased and covered in icing sugar. Sift the remaining icing sugar over the marshmallows and mix slowly with your greased spatula until a dough forms. Transfer the dough onto a greased surface to knead with your hands until the icing sugar and marshmallows are completely blended and the fondant appears to have little to no moisture remaining in it.
- Wrap your ball of fondant 3 or 4 times around with plastic wrap. If you are using it the same day it's good to let it rest on the table at room temperature for 1 hour, but if you are using it later, keep it in the fridge

and take it out of the fridge an hour before you plan to use it.
The fondant can be kept in the fridge for a month and for about six months in the freezer.

- Making fondant is something that takes practice. Even if you've made it successfully once it doesn't mean that the next time is going to work out, but keep practicing and eventually you'll get the hang of it.
- When you're ready to use your fondant, roll it out to roughly ¼ inch thick. Frost your cake with a thin layer of buttercream to give the fondant a surface to stick to. Drape the fondant over your cake, smoothing it out with your hands, and trimming any excess with a knife.
- For your three-layered birthday cake, you'll need to triple this fondant recipe. The sunflower decorations shown in the book were made with fondant and cut out using cookie cutters from a baking supply store. The white icing decorating the cake shown is called royal icing and can be made at home using icing sugar and egg whites, or purchased in tubes at a baking supply store.

Remember, it's always best to use your own imagination!

BUTTERCREAM MIXTURE

Ingredients
5oz softened butter
10oz icing sugar
1-2 tbsp milk
Food coloring (when desired)

Instructions
Beat the butter in a bowl until soft.
Beat in half of the icing sugar until smooth. Then add the remaining icing sugar and one tablespoon of milk and beat the mixture until smooth and creamy.
When necessary, beat in more milk, to loosen the mixture.
Add the food coloring when needed.

Elsa & Anna's
Sunflower Cupcakes

Cupcakes are so fun and easy that everyone can make them! These cupcakes are inspired by Anna and Elsa's favorite spring-time colors. Make them as shown, or use your imagination to make these cupcakes your own!

WHAT YOU NEED

For the vanilla cupcakes:

3 cups sifted cake flour

1½ cups all-purpose flour

2¼ tsp baking powder

1½ tsp coarse salt

¾ tsp baking soda

9 oz unsalted butter, softened

2¼ cups sugar

5 eggs (+ 3 large yolks)

2 cups buttermilk

2 tsp pure vanilla extract

ANNA'S VANILLA CUPCAKES

- Preheat oven to 350°F degrees. Line standard muffin tins with paper liners. Whisk dry ingredients in a large bowl. Cream butter and sugar with a mixer until light and fluffy. Add eggs, 1 at a time, beating after each addition.

- Reduce the speed of your mixer to low. Mix remaining wet ingredients in a bowl. Add dry ingredients to butter mixture in 3 parts, alternating with wet ingredients and ending with dry. Scrape the sides of the bowl. Divide the batter among the muffin cups, filling each completely.

- Bake the cupcakes until a toothpick inserted into the center comes out clean, about 20 minutes. Let cool in tins on wire racks.

- Make the buttercream mixture and put it in a piping bag and put it on the cupcakes.

FLOWERS FOR THE CUPCAKES

The flowers are made from fondant. For futher information on making fondant see page 30.

- Preheat oven to 350°F degrees. Line standard muffin tins with paper liners. Whisk together cocoa and hot water until smooth. In another bowl, whisk together flour, baking soda, baking powder, and salt.

- Melt the butter with the sugar in a saucepan over medium-low heat, stirring to combine. Remove from heat, and pour into a mixing bowl. With an electric mixer on medium-low speed, beat until mixture is cooled, 4 to 5 minutes. Add eggs, one at a time, beating until each is incorporated, scraping down the sides of the bowl as needed. Add vanilla, then the cocoa mixture, and beat until combined. Reduce speed to low. Add the flour mixture in two batches, alternating with the sour cream, beating separately until combined.

- Divide the batter evenly among lined cups, filling each ¾ full. Bake, rotating tins halfway through, until a toothpick inserted in the cupcake centers comes out clean, about 20 minutes. Transfer tins to wire racks to cool for 15 minutes. It´s better to let them cool completely before putting the butter cream on them.

ELSA'S CHOCOLATE CUPCAKES

WHAT YOU NEED

For the chocolate cupcakes:

¾ cup cocoa powder

¾ cup hot water

3 cups all-purpose flour

1 tsp baking soda

1 tsp baking powder

1¼ tsp coarse salt

1½ cups (3 sticks) unsalted butter

2¼ cups sugar

4 large eggs

1 tbsp pure vanilla extract

1 cup sour cream

Lemon Bundt Cake

This cake looks more difficult to make than it is!
Try it out and see how fantastic it will look on your party table
and how scrumptious it will taste!

WHAT YOU NEED

2 cups flour

2 tsp baking powder

2 tsp baking soda

6 eggs

14 tbsp oil

1 ¼ cups caster sugar

6 tbsp soft butter

2 tsp vanilla extract

4 tsp lemon extract

Juice from 1 fresh lemon

Zest from 1 fresh lemon

INSTRUCTIONS

- Preheat the oven to 325°F degees.

- In a large bowl, whisk together eggs, sugar, butter, lemon and vanilla extracts, lemon juice and lemon zest until very well combined or for at least 2-3 minutes.

- In another bowl bring together the dry ingredients. Mix the dry ingredients with the wet ingredients slowly until well combined. Finally, mix in the oil.

- Grease a bundt cake mold and pour in the batter. Bake for 40 minutes or until a toothpick inserted in the cake comes out clean.

- Let it cool for an hour, then sift icing sugar over the cake like snow.

Note: For a healthier option try switching out the wheat for wholewheat or spelt and use dates instead of sugar

Arendelle Spring Nectar

Your party guests need something to drink and this spring nectar is the perfect beverage! It looks and tastes like bottled springtime!

WHAT YOU NEED

Mineral water

Green food coloring

Ice cubes

Lemon water flavoring

INSTRUCTIONS

Mix together mineral water and the lemon water flavoring as instructions say on the packaging and let it rest. After ten minutes mix in the food coloring and put into a beautiful glass bowl to serve with lots of ice cubes.

Olaf's Snowgie Ice Pops

Everybody loves Olaf and in *Frozen Fever* we got more than we bargained for of little snowgies. Even though Olaf loves the sun, he sure is in his element making these delicious ice pops!

What You Need

1 ¾ cups Greek yogurt

¾ cup milk

¼ cup agave syrup
(or 20 drops of Stevia®)

Blue food coloring
(amount depends on the desired color)

Wooden sticks

Ice pop forms

Step 1

Put the Greek yogurt, milk, syrup (or Stevia®) and food coloring into a food processor and blend well.

Step 2

Pour the yogurt mixture into the popsicle forms and place them in the freezer.
Note: If the mixture is too thick, add a little more milk to the batch.

Step 3

After an hour put a wooden stick into each ice pop and return to the freezer overnight or longer, if needed.

OLAF & THE SNOWGIES

Olaf and the snowgies are made with fondant and marshmallows. For futher information on making fondant see page 30.

They take patience to make, but it´s so much fun! Everyone can be a part of the process, and remember, there is no wrong way to do it.

Sven's Fruit Salad

What is better, after a long and hard winter, than a great fruit salad?
This one is as easy to make as it is delicious

WHAT YOU NEED

Assorted fruit:

Green apples

Watermelons

Honeydew melons

Oranges

Pears

Pomegranate seeds

Mint leaves

INSTRUCTIONS

- Wash the fruit thoroughly in luke warm water and dry with a paper towel.

- Slice the apples, melons and pears into medium sized parts. Be sure to remove the core from the apples and pears. Remove the seeds from the melons.

- Peel the orange and take the segments apart.

- Slice the pomegranate in two and take out the seeds and put them with the other sliced fruit.

- Arrange the fruit onto a nice dish or bowl and decorate with mint leaves.

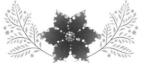

Games

No gathering is complete without party games, and a party in Arendelle is no exception! Can you catch all the snowgies or find the jewels? Can your taste buds handle the dreaded Lemon Taste? Will you find your way in the *Frozen Fever* Scavenger Hunt? This chapter will help you create a memorable party filled with fun activities for your guests.

The Dreaded Lemon Taste

How sensitive are your tastebuds? More importantly, how well can you control your facial expressions? This game will put you to the test!

What You Need

Lemons
or lemon juice

Small plastic
cups

A napkin

Water

Brave
party guests

Instructions

- This game is not for the faint of heart. You must be brave and fearless, for the Dreaded Lemon Taste will test your facial control to the limit.

- Prearrange four drinking cups with water, but add a hefty amount of lemon juice into one of them. Make sure that that cup does not look any different from the others. Cover the cups with a napkin.

- Split the party guests (those brave enough to participate) into groups of four.

- Place the first group in front of the cups in any order. It does not matter which guest is in front of the lemon cup.

- Remove the napkins and instruct the participants to drink all the water in their glass in one large gulp (be sure not to put too much water in each cup).

- If the guest, that drinks the lemon, shows any facial expression, then he/she is out of the game. Participants that don't show any facial expressions are asked to sit aside and participate in the next round. Be sure to have another party guest as a neutral referee.
  Note: The participants must not make any noise either.

- Repeat this as many times as neccesary until you have four finalists (or fewer, depending on how long the game takes).
  The last contestant wins a lemon.

Catch the Snowgies!

Are you as quick on your feet as the fun, little snowgies?
They are tiny and they move fast! Catch them if you can.

What You Need

10 rubber or ping pong balls

A black maker

Super fast party guests

A hard surface floor with some space

Instructions

- Draw a snowgie face (see picture) on 10 rubber or ping pong balls and put them in a basket.

- Split the party guests into teams of four.

- An adult, standing on a chair with the basket of snowgie balls, pours them down to the floor. They will bounce and bounce while one team will have 15 seconds to gather as many snowgie balls as possible. **Note:** The snowgie balls must still be in the air for a qualified catch. If a ball has stopped on the surface then it is out of play.

- Each team will take one turn. The team with the most snowgies wins. If there is a tie, take another turn until there is a winner.

The Frozen Fever
Music Game

The hit single *Making Today a Perfect Day* from *Frozen Fever* is an excellent choice of song for this game of catch the chair.

WHAT YOU NEED

The single *Making Today a Perfect Day* from *Frozen Fever*

A CD/Digital player

Chairs

INSTRUCTIONS

- Arrange a number of chairs depending on how many guests are playing the game. Be sure to have one chair less than the players.Place the chairs side by side in a circle facing out.
  Note: It is best to play this game outside. You will need the space.

- The players stand in front of the chairs. Once the music starts playing the players must walk steadily around the circle of chairs.

- The music suddenly stops and all the players must scramble to sit down on one of the chairs. The player without a seat is out of the game. Remember to remove one chair after each round.

- Repeat until one player is left sitting in the last chair.

  Note: The one who controls the music must remember to vary the length of time the music is played. Keep the players guessing!

The Quest for Olaf

How much do you know about Arendelle and the Frozen world? Would you be able to navigate through a scavenger hunt by following Frozen clues? Soon we will see, for Olaf is lost and it is time for a quest.

What You Need

5-6 different riddles

5-6 different clues

Colored paper

A picture of Olaf

Instructions

- Split the guests into two competing groups. Group One is Elsa's and Sven's. Group Two is Anna's and Kristoff's. Both groups want to find Olaf as soon as possible!

- Before the party, start planning the Quest for Olaf in detail. Plant at least 5 clues or riddles in various locations around the neighborhood. The difficulty level can vary but try to keep the locations in the near vicinity of your home. Be sure to choose locations that most of the guests recognize. *It is also prudent to have one grown-up accompany each group.*

- You can decorate the clues in various colored paper, but be sure to assign different colors to each group. That way there is no confusion if both groups get to the same place at the same time.

- Base the riddles on *Frozen Fever*. Here are a few helpful suggestions:
  Note: Where there is a riddle one adult must be present to read the riddle and receive an answer.

  Riddle 1: Who's birthday is it in *Frozen Fever*?
  Answer: Anna's.

  Riddle 2: Who gets sick?
  Answer: Elsa.

Riddle 3: Where do the snowgies end up?
Answer: In Elsa's ice palace!

Riddle 4: How many snowgies are there?
Answer: We don't know. (Any answer is correct)

- Contestants must answer these, or other, questions correctly. An adult then gives the group directions to the next location. If they do not have the answer they must wait for 1 minute before continuing.

- **Clues:** When contestants arrive at a location they will find a note or a package in their team colors. There they will get clues or instructions to the next location.
Note: The person throwing the party has to be sure every instruction or clue is based on the contestants knowledge of the surrounding neighborhood.

- The first team to solve all the riddles or follow all the clues is the winner!

The Magic Jewel Hunt

Remember the gorgeous jewel bracelet invitations you learned to make earlier in the book? Well, in this game they'll be put to good use. Who will end up with all the jewels?

WHAT YOU NEED

The Jewel
Invitation
from page 8

INSTRUCTIONS

- Before the party starts choose 2 words that the players of this game should not say when playing the game. The 2 words will be the same for everyone playing. Choose words that are often used and easy to remember, like "no," "maybe," or "red."

- When greeting your guests at the party you ask for their Jewel Invitation from page 8. Tie the bracelet around the guest's wrist while reciting this phrase: "Guard these jewels well!" You then give each guest the 2 words they cannot say throughout the whole party.

- All the party guests now have the task of making the other guests say those forbidden words.

- If a party guest succeeds in getting another to say a forbidden word she gets a jewel from that guest.

- This game goes on for the duration of the party. The guest with the most jewels in the end wins.
  Note: If a guest has lost all her colored jewels she need not despair. She can still play the game and try to win more jewels!

Party Favors

Send your guests off with their their hearts filled with fun memories and holding a specially-made party favor that they can have for a keepsake.

Olaf's Party Favor Packaging

Olaf is a fountain of creative ideas and here is one of them, a fun way to package and decorate your party favor!

WHAT YOU NEED

White paper bags

Waterproof markers (black/orange)

Orange gouache paint

Paintbrush

See-through paper

Clothespins

A party favor

STEP 1

When choosing the size of the white paper bag, be sure to have it in proportion to the clothespin.

STEP 2

Cut out a piece of see-through paper large enough to write a farewell message to your party guest.
Put aside for the moment while the marker is drying.

STEP 3

Paint the clothespins orange and set aside to dry entirely.

STEP 4

Take the paper bag and draw Olaf's face with the black marker (see picture). Let it dry.

STEP 5

To inflate the bag a bit put some crumpled newspaper in the bottom. Place the thank you note in the bottom of the bag and add the party favor on top of it. Fold the top of the paper bag (see picture) and fasten it with the orange clothespin. Olaf's Party Favor Packaging is done!

Arendelle's Candle of Peace

This is a simple yet beautiful party favor that sends a good message as well! Have fun designing these or use them as inspiration!

What You Need

Small cardboard box

Small candles

Cotton wool

Silver glitter dust

Flower template from page 60

Note: This treat may not be suitable for very young guests and it is always safest to give this to the child under parental supervision.

Step 1

Create a flower decoration using the template on page 60. Be sure it fits on the lid of the box. Use any colors to create a beautiful decoration.

Step 2

Place some cotton wool in the container and then put the candle on top. Sprinkle with silver glitter dust.

Step 3

If desired, add a snowgie made from fondant and marshmallows as shown on page 30. Close with the decorated lid.

Templates

YOU ARE INVITED TO   FROZEN FEVER PARTY!

WHEN _____

WHERE _____

RSVP _____

Copy image 100%

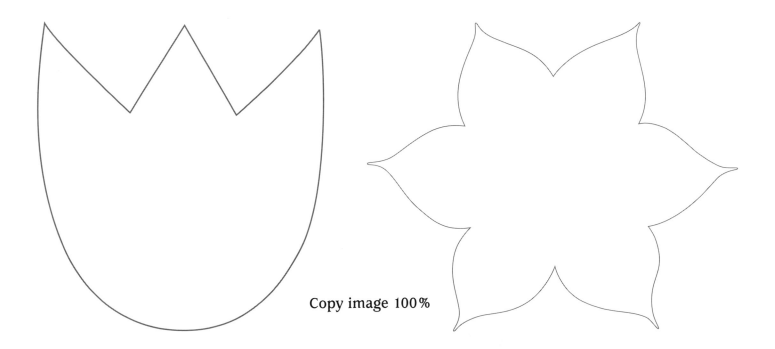

Copy image 100%

Enlarge image 150%

Table corner edge

Enlarge image 200% or as desired.

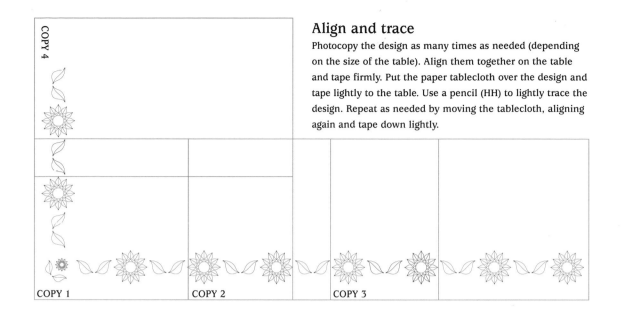

Align and trace

Photocopy the design as many times as needed (depending on the size of the table). Align them together on the table and tape firmly. Put the paper tablecloth over the design and tape lightly to the table. Use a pencil (HH) to lightly trace the design. Repeat as needed by moving the tablecloth, aligning again and tape down lightly.

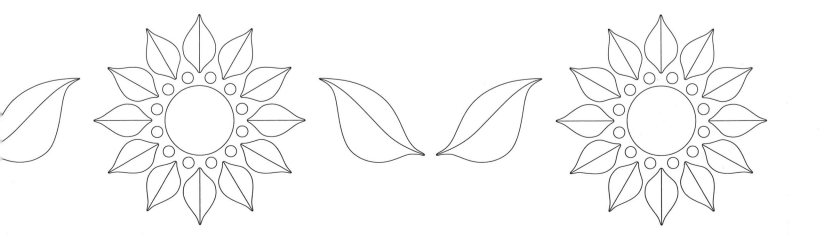

Index